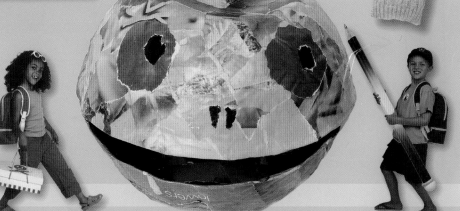

Don't throw it away— create something amazing!

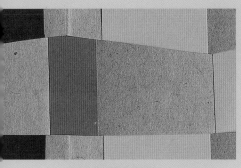

DK

LONDON, NEW YORK, MUNICH,
MELBOURNE, AND DELHI

For **Stephen**

DESIGN • Jane Bull
EDITOR • Penelope Arlon
PHOTOGRAPHY • Andy Crawford
DESIGNER • Gemma Fletcher

PUBLISHING MANAGER • Sue Leonard
ART DIRECTOR • Rachael Foster
PRODUCTION EDITOR • Sean Daly

First published in the United States in 2008 by
DK Publishing
375 Hudson Street, New York, New York 10014

08 09 10 11 12 10 9 8 7 6 5 4 3 2 1
ND117 - 03/08

A CIP record for this book
is available from the Library of Congress

ISBN: 978-0-7566-3837-5
Color reproduction by MDP, UK
Printed and bound by Mohn Media, Germany

Are you ready to recycle?

Mixed Sources
Product group from well-managed
forests and other controlled sources
www.fsc.org Cert no. SA-COC-1592
© 1996 Forest Stewardship Council
FSC

discover more at
www.dk.com

Make it!

Here's what's in the book...

From Trash...

Looking for materials? These come **FREE** to you every day—so don't dump valuable stuff. Use it to make something new—RECYCLE IT, and help the planet, too!

Throw away?
NO WAY!

Did you know? Most of our garbage gets buried in the ground...

...or burned.

All this stuff costs money to make and costs the Earth, too.

STARVE YOUR GARBAGE CAN
Recycle!

Don't throw me away. I'm **plastic** so I'll last a lifetime!

Don't fork out for new materials—you get me for FREE! USE ME AGAIN and again and again...

If all this trash gets buried, it really will be **"buried treasure."**

It's crazy! Don't bury garbage. It doesn't go away!

...to TREASURE

Make
something
NEW

So DON'T TRASH it—TREASURE it!

The 3 "Rs" to recycling

It's not all garbage—about half the stuff we throw in the trash can be recycled. Remember the three "Rs" and help to keep garbage out of landfill sites and incinerators.

Why should you do the 3 "Rs"?

Watch how much garbage your family throws out each week—it will surprise you. All that garbage has to go somewhere and that somewhere is an incinerator where it is burned, or a landfill site where it is buried. A lot of what we put in landfill sites, such as plastic, will remain there for hundreds of years. There is a famous landfill in New York City called *Fresh Kills* that is now so big, it has become the largest man-made structure in the world.

What if you don't?

If we continue to throw away as much garbage as we do now, landfill sites will get bigger and bigger, and burning garbage causes air pollution and toxic ashes. We all need clean air and water to survive, and if we don't reduce, reuse, and recycle, we will damage our world. Help our planet be a healthy place to live, not just for people, but for animals and plants as well.

Reduce

Means finding ways to cut down on garbage. Don't accept plastic bags from stores—take your own bag.

Reuse

Means finding ways to use things again and again and again without throwing them away.

Close the circle

Try to buy more products made from recycled material to help to close the circle.

Recycle

Means taking something old and turning it into something new.

! Ask an ADULT
Watch out, you may need some help along the way in this book.

YOU can help

Here are ideas for things you can do to help.

• Buy items with little or no packaging. This will reduce your garbage.

• Refill your water bottles and keep reusing them.

• Buy, sell, or donate your things. Don't throw them away—help a charity.

• Use both sides of a sheet of paper before recycling it.

• Get the family involved—recycling only works if everyone joins in.

• Find out about recycling in your area, then use your local recycling center.

Sort your stuff

In this book the materials are divided into four sections—paper, plastic, metal, and fabric.

Know your stuff

To help you understand why it's important to recycle materials, it helps to know some facts about them. Look for the "Know your stuff" circles that appear in this book.

KNOW YOUR STUFF
Facts about a material. They appear throughout the book.

Start recycling

• Use different containers for each material.
• Some packaging is made of more than one material, so make sure you separate materials before you recycle.
• Before you toss anything, make sure you can't reuse it first.

Paper

Newspapers
Wrapping paper
Magazines
Envelopes
Comics
Cardboard boxes
Cartons

Plastic

Drink bottles
Straws
Bottle tops
Carrier bags
Toys

Metal

Foil wrap
Foil food trays
Food cans
Paper clips
Safety pins
Soft-drink cans
Paper fasteners
Wire

Fabric

T-shirts
Cotton skirts
Denim jeans
Woolen socks and gloves
Nylon tights
Ribbon

Try recycling your paper to make these scrap pots.

Paper—the best invention in the world!

We paint on it, we read and write on it, we can fold it into shapes, we can wrap presents in it, and much, much more.

Paper

Imagine our world without paper—that would mean no letters, no cardboard packaging, no newspapers, no wrapping paper, and no toilet paper!

What is paper made from?

Most of the paper we use is made from trees. Billions of pine trees are cut down every year to make our paper.

When was paper invented?

Paper has been around for thousands of years. The ancient Egyptians made it from the papyrus plant. That's where we got the word paper.

How is paper made?

The trees are chopped up into little pieces called chips. They are then made into a mushy pulp and a lot of chemicals and water are added. The pulp is then rolled flat into paper.

Paper gets thrown away more than any other material.

Think about how many newspapers are made every day that end up as trash.

Paper uses

We use paper all the time. Count how many times you come across paper in one day. You'll be surprised by how much there is out there. Now imagine how many trees have been cut down to make it.

Look for the symbol

Try to buy recycled paper—look for this symbol; you'll find it on anything from cartons and stationery to toilet-paper rolls.

Recycled paper

Recycled paper contains fewer chemicals and bleaches than brand-new paper, and it saves trees, too. A piece of paper can't be recycled forever, however, because the fibers will start to break down. High-grade paper can be remade into newspapers and magazines and these can go on to become egg cartons.

Magic folds

How can you turn a flat, flimsy piece of paper into a strong box? Can you make paper fly? Try your hand at some paper-folding magic.

Try different paper sizes for big or small boxes.

Try out newspaper, comics, and colored paper.

This paper is amazing stuff.

Perform some PAPER magic

Fold and hold—just a few folds and tucks and a flat piece of paper becomes a sturdy box. That's paper magic!

Fold a rectangle of paper in half, and half again four times, to make 16 squares. Then unfold it.

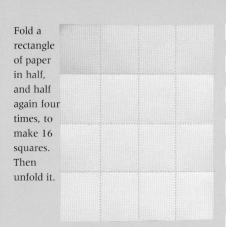

Bring the top and bottom flaps into the center.

Fold each corner down two-thirds to the center.

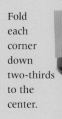

Fold up the two flaps so the corners are tucked in.

Hold the center of the two sides and pull them apart.

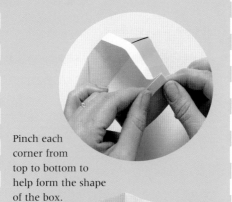

Pinch each corner from top to bottom to help form the shape of the box.

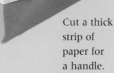

Cut a thick strip of paper for a handle.

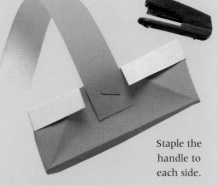

Staple the handle to each side.

Try using patterned paper or paint a piece yourself.

Watch paper fly!

Paper plane—a few simple folds and it flies!

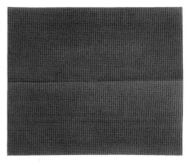

Take a rectangle of paper and fold it in half.

Turn down one corner, as shown.

Fold the same corner down again.

Now fold the top part down to make a wing.

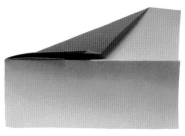

Now make the other wing

Repeat the folds on the other half of the paper.

Open out the wings turn the plane over, and whizz it across the room!

Pumpkin pot.

Scrap paper pots

Paper is everywhere.

Just think about how much is thrown away each day. Why not turn your scraps into funky paper pots.

Look for scraps of the same color for a solid look.

Tree frog pot.

Magazine scraps make colorful pots.

The frog pot is made of lots of pictures of trees from magazines.

KNOW YOUR STUFF

Recycled magazines and comics can be molded into paper products like egg cartons.

The insides of envelopes make up this scrap pot......

Envelope pot

Candy wrappers give this pot a shiny look...

Tissue pot...

Candy pot

Torn tissue paper gives a great ragged effect.........

Comic pot

Tear up favorite comic strips for a cartoon pot....

Homemade paste

This simple homemade paste works really well with your paper projects, and the good news is it's completely eco-friendly. Your projects can be recycled afterward because the ingredients are natural. This paste works best when it's fresh so make a new batch for each project.

You will need:

1 cup flour

+

3 cups water

! **Ask an ADULT** to help heat up the saucepan.

1.

Put one cup of water and one cup of flour into a saucepan.

.....Stir with a wooden spoon until the mixture is smooth.

2.

Keep stirring!

......Add the rest of the water and bring the mixture to the boil, stirring all the time. Then turn off the heat.

3.

Homemade paste

Pour into a bowl and allow to cool.

NOW IT'S READY TO USE!

Make a newspaper pot

Use your homemade paste. You will also need petroleum jelly, a plastic bowl, and lots of old torn-up newspaper. For your pot and lid, make two bowls which you can decorate when they are dry.

Grease a bowl with petroleum jelly to stop the paper from sticking to it.....

Petroleum jelly

Tear up lots and lots of newspaper strips, about 1 x 2 in (2 x 4 cm). .....

1.

.....Place a layer of paper directly onto the greased bowl.

2.

.....Brush on a layer of paste.

3.

Add another layer of paper.....

4.

.....Keep adding the paste and paper until you have about six layers.

5.

Leave the bowl to dry out completely.....

6.

Remove the bowl and trim off the rough edge. .....

Decorate your scrap pots

When your two bowls are dry, start decorating. One bowl will be the base and the other will be the lid. Use the homemade paste to stick on any colorful strips of paper.

Paste the outside and inside.

Experiment with different types of paper.

Tear up pieces of colored paper and cover your pot with them.

Tear out circles to make a frog face.

Paste them in place.

! **Ask an ADULT** to help you make a slit in the lid.

Make a tissue bowl

Make a tissue bowl the same way as the newspaper bowl— just use tissue paper instead.

Make a handle

To add a handle, ask an adult to make a slit in the lid. Cut out a strip of thick paper, about 3 x 1 in (7 x 2 cm), and fold it in the middle. Push it through the lid and tape it in place on the inside.

Leave to dry completely before removing the bowl.

Tear up pieces of tissue paper.

Grease the bowl.

Add a layer of tissue paper, then using the paste, build up about 10–12 layers.

Junk mail mâché

Envelopes

Fliers

Brown paper

Paper is delivered to your door every day—for free! Don't just chuck it, save it up and make some junk mail mâché.

Gift wrap

Advertisements

Free Magazines

Magazines

Little bits of junk mail

KNOW YOUR STUFF
If you don't use your junk mail, make sure you recycle it.

Envelopes

Think before you throw away envelopes. Greeting cards come in all kinds of colored ones.

Junk mail

Sort through your junk mail and keep the bright pieces. Remember to recycle the rest!

Paper boy

Color pots

Sort your scraps into colors and you can make single color pots.

Pots as presents

How to make junk mail mâché

Tearing and mulching

The great thing about junk mail mâché is that it gets really messy! So roll up your sleeves and dive in.

Start by tearing lots of paper into tiny pieces. You can sort them into colors or mix them up.

1.

Fill a plastic bowl with your paper pieces. Pour in hot water.

! Ask an ADULT to help with the hot water.

2.

Make sure the hot water covers the paper.

3.

Leave the paper for three hours. Then drain away the water through a strainer.

Squeeze the paper as dry as you can.

4.

Spoon some eco paste (see page 16) into your mixture, then mix it with your hands until it's a gluey mulch. Tear up the paper some more as you work.

How to make mâché bowls

Now it's time to spread the mulch around a plastic bowl. Do it bit by bit instead of putting the whole bunch in at once.

Rub some petroleum jelly all over the inside of a plastic bowl. This will stop the mulch from sticking.

1.

2.

Press your mulch hard to the inside of the bowl.

3.

Don't worry if you leave holes here and there; this adds to the character!

4.

Leave it to dry overnight or until it is really hard and dry. Use a knife to loosen carefully around the edge of the bowl.

5.

Lift it out and fill it up with goodies!

Junk mail jewels

Your junk mail mâché can also be made into fantastic jewels.

Cookie cutters

Cookie-cutter shapes

Place a cookie cutter on a piece of plastic to keep it from sticking. Take a small amount of damp mâché and press it into the cutter. Push the shape out onto a sheet of paper towel. Then make a hole for some string, and leave to dry.

Press the mâché firmly inside the cookie shape.

Make the hole with a toothpick.

Push out onto the paper.

Paper towel

Piece of plastic

22

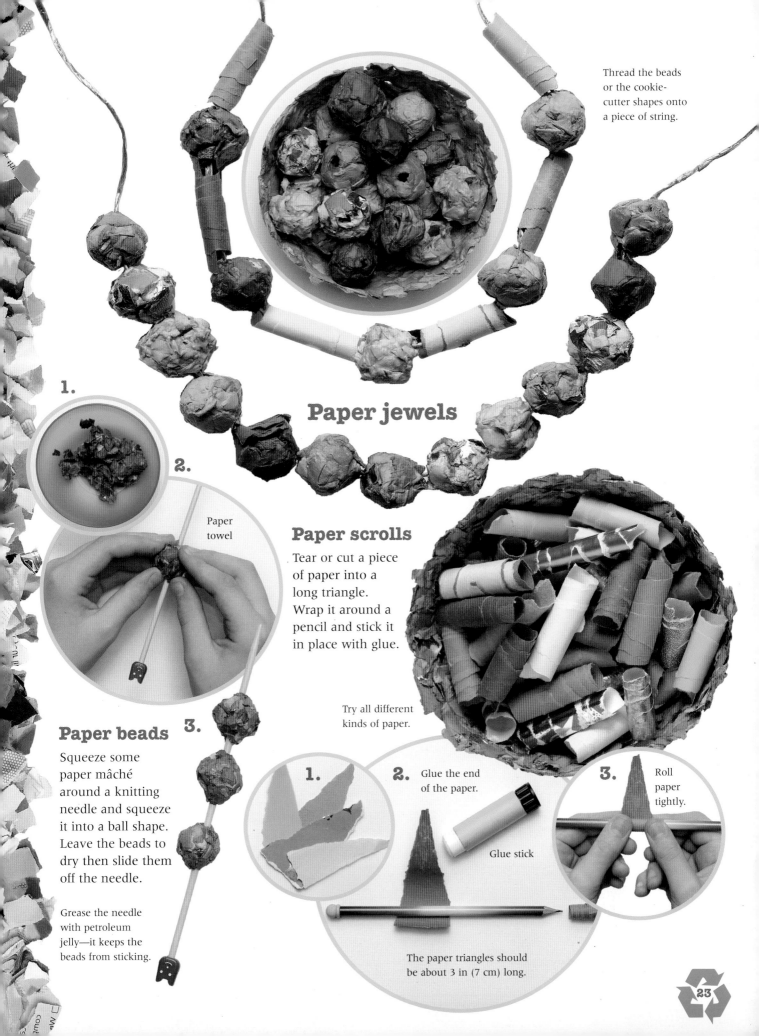

Thread the beads or the cookie-cutter shapes onto a piece of string.

1.

2.

Paper towel

Paper jewels

Paper scrolls

Tear or cut a piece of paper into a long triangle. Wrap it around a pencil and stick it in place with glue.

Try all different kinds of paper.

Paper beads

3.

Squeeze some paper mâché around a knitting needle and squeeze it into a ball shape. Leave the beads to dry then slide them off the needle.

Grease the needle with petroleum jelly—it keeps the beads from sticking.

1.

2. Glue the end of the paper.

Glue stick

3. Roll paper tightly.

The paper triangles should be about 3 in (7 cm) long.

Paper weaving

Under, over, under, over. Don't throw paper away, turn it into art. Weave pictures and turn them into cards or stick them on the wall.

1. Take an envelope and cut along the short sides and one long side. Cut off the flap too.

2. Now when you open it out you should have a large sheet of paper, like this.

3. Fold the paper in half again and draw evenly spaced lines down the sheet.

4. Cut the strips from the folded edge but STOP before you get to the top.

5. Open the sheet out. Under, over, under, over, until you get to the end. Remember to start the next strip in the opposite way— over, under, over, under.

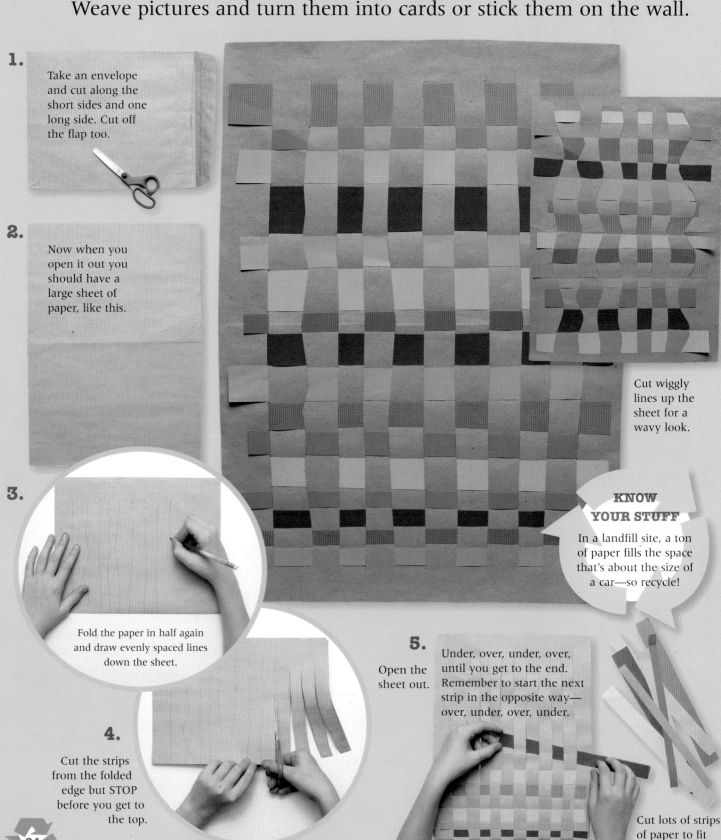

Cut wiggly lines up the sheet for a wavy look.

KNOW YOUR STUFF

In a landfill site, a ton of paper fills the space that's about the size of a car—so recycle!

Cut lots of strips of paper to fit across the width of the sheet.

24

Under, over, under, over, weave, weave, weave

Picture weave

Try using a picture from a magazine as your backing sheet, then weave plain strips along it.

Weave art

Experiment with your weaving by using pictures or patterns as well as plain paper. Use any paper you can find.

Turn your weaves into colorful cards.

Try patterned strips and a plain background.

This weave uses the inside of envelopes.

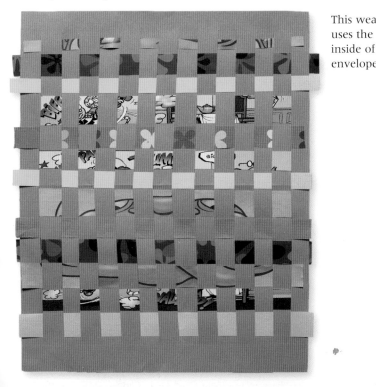

Paper portraits

Picture in a box

Turn old pictures into new ones—then frame them in a box.

KNOW YOUR STUFF
Recycling a 3 ft (1 m) stack of flattened boxes can SAVE ONE TREE.

Box frames

Stop your family from throwing away old food boxes.

You will need:

• A cereal box
• Lots of pictures, postcards, junk mail, and colorful patterns from old magazines.

Draw a line around the edge of the front of the box leaving a 1 in (2 cm) rim. Then cut it out.

1. Use the piece of cardboard you cut out of the box as your picture.

Glue stick

Tear strips of blue paper as a sea background and glue them on. It doesn't have to look neat. Try different shades of blue for a stormy effect.

2. Glue scraps roughly for a 3-D effect.

Now cut or tear pieces of paper—keeping the shape of some objects but tearing others roughly to create a textured edge.

Attach a few shapes using a card strip so they stand away from the picture and looks 3-D.

3.

When you have glued your picture, you may want to make a border around the edge with extra pieces of torn paper.

Slip your picture inside your box and glue it to the back.

Take a closer look—can you tell what the pictures used to be?

Corn field

Blue towel

Chocolate hair

Rubber gloves

Carpet face

Grass

Car bonnet shirt

Number

Letters   Red towel   Coffee beans   Pizza   Apples   Let the tissue paper flap over for a wavy plant look.

27

Reuse your plastic odds and ends and have yourself a plastic party!

Plastic—it's fantastic!

It can be shiny, smooth, rough, tough, hard, or soft. It can be any color, AND it can be molded into any shape.

Plastic

Imagine our world without plastic—there would be no plastic toys, plastic packaging, or plastic telephones. Plastic is easy to make BUT it's not so easy to get rid of.

What is plastic made from?

Like paper, plastic comes from trees. Some smart scientists got a substance called cellulose out of wood pulp and that made plastic.

When was it invented?

In 1862 a British chemist called Alexander Parkes was experimenting with cellulose. He heated it, molded it, and found that when it cooled, it kept its shape. Plastic was born.

Plastic today

After pulping wood to get plastic, chemists started creating it in laboratories. They use chemicals to make plastics such as polyethylene and polystyrene.

Plastic problem

DID YOU KNOW? If you lined up all the foam plastic cups made in a day, they would reach around the Earth.

Plastic uses

Take a look around your bedroom—you can probably spot at least 10 pieces of plastic. Perhaps you have a CD player— and what about all your pens and toy animals?

Look for the symbols

Most plastic items you buy have a symbol on them. The PETE 1 symbol is the one to watch for.

Recycling plastic PETE 1

PETE 1 plastic, which is found in most drink bottles, can be recycled easily. It can be turned into clothing, stuffing for sleeping bags, stuffed toys, rulers, and lots, lots more. So make sure you recycle all your water and soft-drink bottles.

Rainbow frame

Plastic comes in so many great colors—so gather all those tiny plastic bits and pieces and make one of these fantastic plastic frames.

Now they look as pretty as a picture.

KNOW YOUR STUFF
Don't bury your plastic—it'll be there for hundreds of years.

1. Tidy up your toys

Sort your plastic odds and ends into rainbow colors.

Things look neat already!

2. Make a frame

Use cardboard from an old box.

! **Ask an ADULT** to help cut out a frame shape.

3. Glue the pieces

Cover it with all your plastic.

Glue the pieces in their color groups.

Crazy ice

Cut the bottoms off plastic bottles, fill them with water, and freeze.

Color the water with food coloring.

Refill Refill Refill

For picnics refill bottles with your own homemade drinks.

KNOW YOUR STUFF

Recycle your bottles—12 of them can be turned into a new fleece top.

Set up 10 bottles and knock them down.

Bowling game

A ball of screwed-up paper will work too...

Mini plant cover

Half a plastic bottle placed over your seedlings will keep them warm and help them grow.

Bottle bank

Plastic bottles

will last for hundreds of years, so it's crazy to only use them once. Here are some ways to reuse them.

Make the most of me!

! Ask an ADULT

to help you cut the bottles. Plastic can be tough.

Bird feeder

Cut a hole in the side of the bottle.

Put a length of string through the bottle neck and tie the end to the lid.

Put seed in the bottom of your bird feeder and hang it up for the birds to snack on.

Pull the string so the lid sits in the neck.

Toy boat

Try any plastic pieces you can find to decorate your boat.

Make sure you keep the lids on the bottles so they will float.

Use a plastic foam tray as the base. Tie the bottles to it.

Sun catcher

Hang your bottle in the sun and watch it sparkle.

To make a fancy edge...

...cut the bottom off a bottle, cut strips up its length, and roll them up.

Rain catcher

Cut a bottle in half, turn the top upside down, and place it back in the bottom half. Now sit it outdoors to catch the rain.

Handy holder

Use a bottle bottom as a pencil holder or even a flower vase.

Cut strips down the bottle and roll each one.

Bottle top art

Lots of bottles means lots of lids. You'll be amazed how they pile up.

1. Use a plastic foam sheet, like a pizza base or foam packaging.

2. Start from the center. Use strong glue to stick the tops to the base.

3. Keep adding to your pattern.

Careful—I could lose my head!

Bottle top patterns

Collect lots of pretty colored lids and make patterns with them. You can hang them on a wall or even use them as place mats or colorful coasters.

Try different designs

KNOW
YOUR STUFF
TOPS OFF when you recycle your plastic bottles. The tops are made of a different plastic, which isn't as easy to recycle.

Bottle-top badges

Collect up your bottle tops and fill them with lots of tiny plastic beads, buttons, and toys.

Adhesive labels

Make sure you clean the lids.

Safety pins

1.

2.

3.

Attach a safety pin to the back of the badge using an adhesive label.

Use strong glue to keep everything in place.

Try matching the colors so each badge has a theme.

Tie and hang

Tie each end of the streamers securely so they don't come undone, then hang them up.

Who knew plastic could be so much fun!

Plastic party

Bottle banners and pen-top streamers brighten up any party. And you don't have to buy decorations at all— just reuse and recycle!

What to use

Next time you are at a party, gather up the used party popper bottles—they're great for streamers. Keep an eye out for pen and bottle lids, clothes pins, and straws, too.

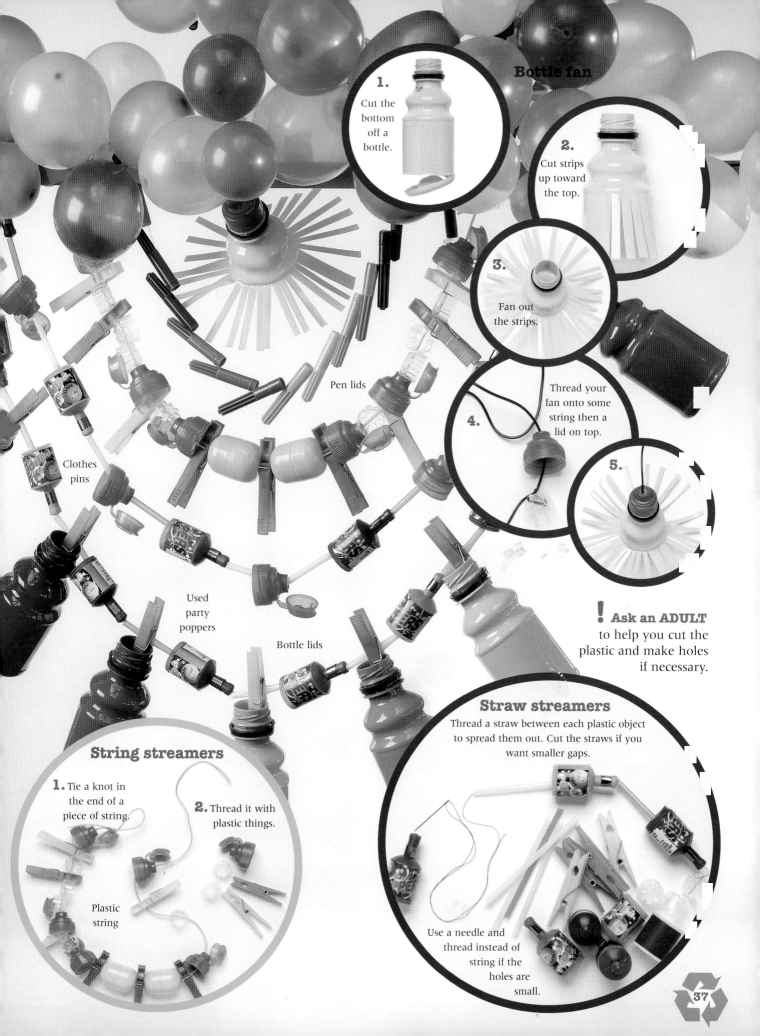

Bottle fan

1. Cut the bottom off a bottle.

2. Cut strips up toward the top.

3. Fan out the strips.

4. Thread your fan onto some string then a lid on top.

5.

Pen lids

Clothes pins

Used party poppers

Bottle lids

! Ask an **ADULT** to help you cut the plastic and make holes if necessary.

Straw streamers

Thread a straw between each plastic object to spread them out. Cut the straws if you want smaller gaps.

String streamers

1. Tie a knot in the end of a piece of string.

2. Thread it with plastic things.

Plastic string

Use a needle and thread instead of string if the holes are small.

37

Plastic wrappers

Brighten up your room. Turn plastic wrappers into a colorful cushion or shiny screen.

Decide how big you want your cushion to be and cut a rectangle double that size out of bubble wrap.

Fold the bubble wrap in half and tape up two of the open sides with adhesive tape.

Stuff the bubble wrap

Bubble-wrap cushions are easy to make, but the real art is in the stuffing. Bubble wrap is see-through, so make sure you stuff it with lots of colorful plastic odds and ends. When you have finished stuffing, tape up the open side.

This will make you comfortable.

KNOW YOUR STUFF
Candy wrappers and potato chip bags make up a huge proportion of what you throw away.

How to make a candy-wrap screen

Take a length of netting material and cut a pole to hang it from. Fold the top of the net over the pole and glue it down. Collect lots of plastic candy wrappers and buttons and start decorating.

Cut the pole long enough to poke out on each side of the net.

Use glue to stick the netting down and to attach the decorations.

Cellophane candy wrappers

You can use an old net curtain for the screen, or the type of netting on a ballet tutu.

Nylon netting material

Plastic buttons

39

Metal—is magical!

It can be shiny and cold, strong, wiry, smooth, or sharp.
It's magnetic, can carry electricity, and it's valuable stuff, too.

Metal

Imagine our world without metal—We wouldn't have any money, jewelry, skyscraper buildings, and we would have a very difficult time cooking without any metal.

COPPER

TIN

ALUMINUM

NICKEL

IRON

GOLD

SILVER

STEEL

What is metal?

All metal comes from rocks in the ground. Rock is broken up and heated to get the metal out.

When was metal discovered?

As far back as 11,000 years ago early people were making tools and jewelry out of metal. Today, we make things like watches, wire, and even spaceships!

How is foil made?

The foil wrap we use in cooking is made of ALUMINUM, which comes from a rock called bauxite. To turn it into foil a block of aluminum is squashed through rollers again and again until it's a long flat sheet.

Who invented the CAN?

A Frenchman, Nicholas Appert, invented the STEEL can in 1810 to preserve food for Napoleon's army.

Metal uses

So many things around you are made from metal or have metal in them. Look around your kitchen—ovens, saucepans, cutlery are all made of metal. That's because it is strong and easy to clean.

Recycle metal

Every time you recycle metal you are saving the Earth from being dug up. Rock that contains metal can't grow back. Once it's dug up, that's it!

Test your metal

Hold a magnet near some cans, you'll find some will stick; these are made of STEEL. **STEEL cans are 100% recyclable.** Most soft-drink cans are made of ALUMINUM, which can be recycled and made into just about anything, from cars to brand-new cans, SO RECYCLE!

Mysterious metal

Test your metal

Find out which metals are magnetic by touching a magnet onto various objects—if it sticks, they're magnetic.

Fishing game

Cut fish shapes out of paper and fasten a paper clip or paper fastener onto them. Tie a magnet onto a piece of string, tie the string to a pencil, then race your friends to pick up the fish.

Moving metal—

Metals are attracted to magnets—that's the magic of metal—so dig out those magnets. Here's how to make metal work for you.

Can do!

Tin cans are great to reuse as storage, and because they are metal, you can decorate them with magnets. You can even spell out what is in them with letter magnets.

! Ask an ADULT

to cut the top off the can. Make sure they clean it and check it for sharp edges.

Homemade fridge magnets

Glue a magnet to the top of a jar or bottle lid, then glue a small toy to the other side. Stick them on the fridge or your storage cans.

Reuse lids from jars.

Magnets

Strong glue

Small toys

Cover a lid with foil.

Make a moving picture

1.

Decorate the background.

Make a base by cutting out a piece of thin cardboard—try using the back of a cereal box.

Crazy Cat—make him dance!

Paper clip whiskers

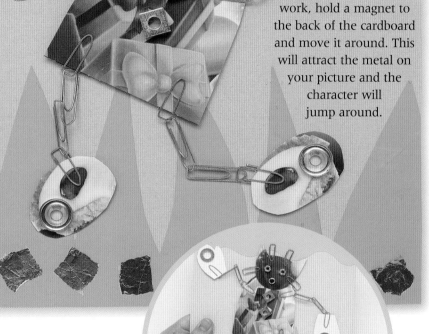

To make the picture work, hold a magnet to the back of the cardboard and move it around. This will attract the metal on your picture and the character will jump around.

2.

Cut out cat shapes from thin cardboard.

Paper fastener

Cut out separate hands and feet.

3.

Paper fastener

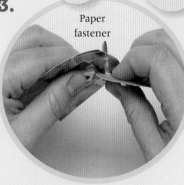

Take a paper fastener and push it through the face to make the cat's nose. Then push it through the body.

BACK OF PICTURE

Attach the cat to the cardboard by pressing the paper fastener through the back of the cardboard.

4.

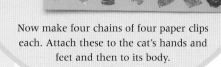

Now make four chains of four paper clips each. Attach these to the cat's hands and feet and then to its body.

Hold the magnet at the back of the cardboard and gently move it around.

Magnet

I'm not magnetic because I'm plastic.

43

Metal Mix-up

Shiny shapes.

Collect lots of shiny metal objects and let them hang, swing, and dangle. Watch the metal glisten and sparkle.

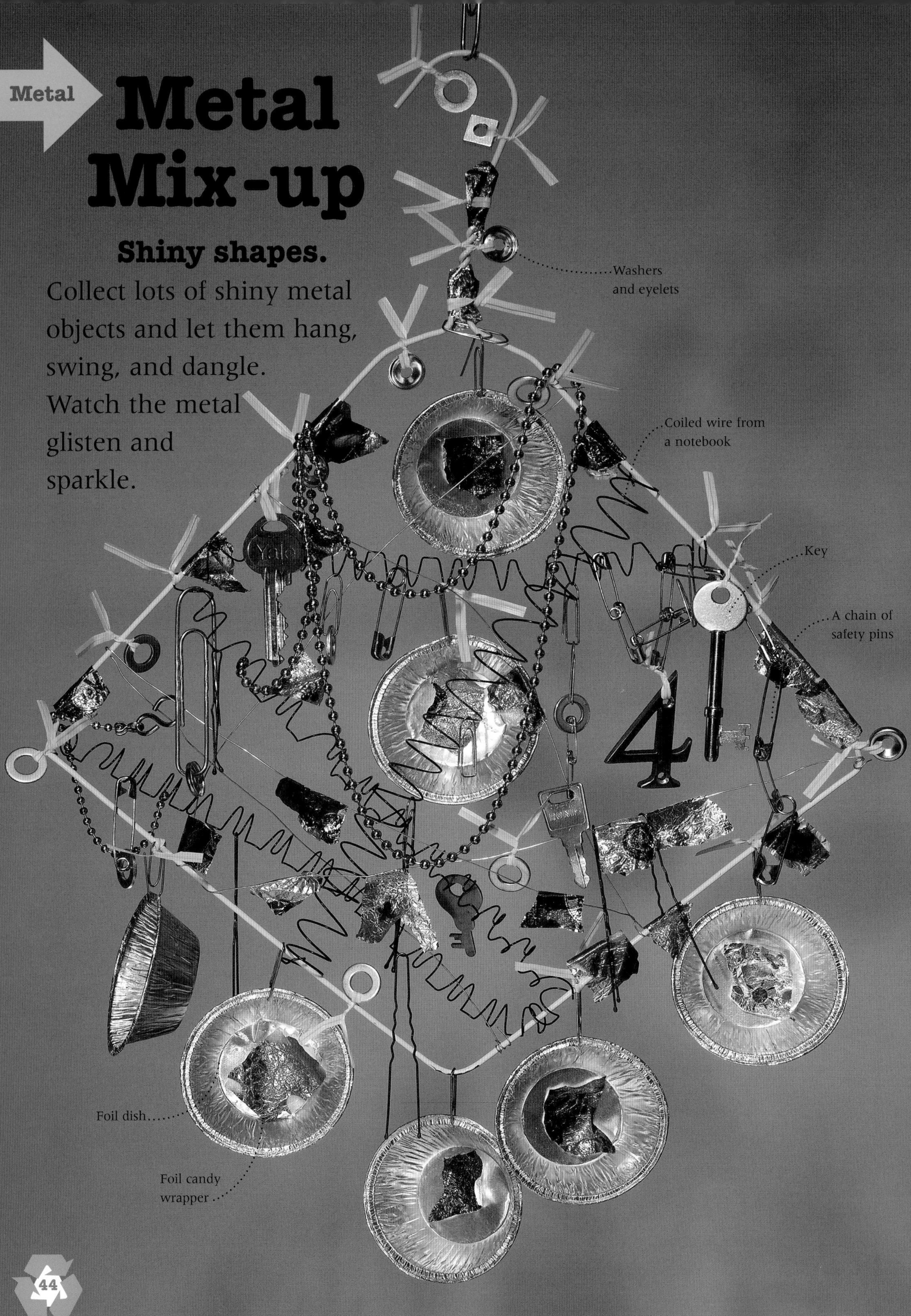

Washers and eyelets

Coiled wire from a notebook

Key

A chain of safety pins

Foil dish

Foil candy wrapper

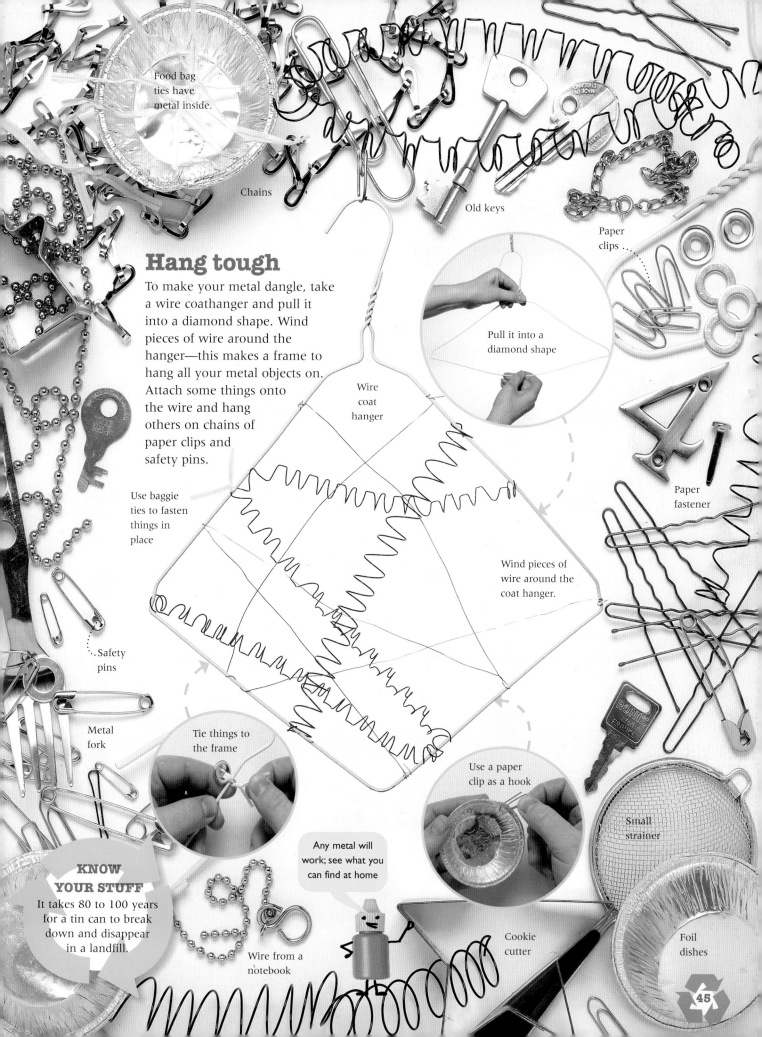

Food bag ties have metal inside.

Chains

Old keys

Paper clips

Hang tough

To make your metal dangle, take a wire coathanger and pull it into a diamond shape. Wind pieces of wire around the hanger—this makes a frame to hang all your metal objects on. Attach some things onto the wire and hang others on chains of paper clips and safety pins.

Pull it into a diamond shape

Wire coat hanger

Use baggie ties to fasten things in place

Wind pieces of wire around the coat hanger.

Paper fastener

Safety pins

Metal fork

Tie things to the frame

Use a paper clip as a hook

Any metal will work; see what you can find at home

Small strainer

Wire from a notebook

Cookie cutter

Foil dishes

45

Make a Mobile

Reuse clean foil dishes and decorate them with candy wrappers and other shiny metal things. Attach paper clips and chains to hang them up.

Glue foil candy wrappers to the foil dishes.

Strong glue

All these trays are made of ALUMINUM.

KNOW YOUR STUFF

Scrunch a candy wrapper into a ball. If it's made of metal foil, it will stay in a ball.

Mirror mobiles

Reflect the light with these simple mobiles. Hang them in a sunny window to shimmer and shine.

Link paper clips together to make a chain.

Glue different-sized dishes together.

Link dishes together with a paper clip.

Pipe cleaners are made of metal too!

Metal models

Space age.

Build metal robots, rockets, and aliens and create a shiny, lunar landscape.

.....Foil dish hat

.....Foil tube head

4.

Glue them together.

Make a model

Foil food trays are a good start for the robot body. Cut down cardboard tubes for the legs and head, and wrap them in aluminum foil. Then use odds and ends for your metal man's features.

1.

Toilet or paper-towel roll tubes can be covered in foil.

Wrap them up tightly.

Pipe cleaner arms.

Use strong glue to attach his face and buttons.

2.

Tape the tube legs to the tray.

3.

Tape the arms on to the tray.

Space rocket

Tape a foil dish to the base. ....

Wrap a soft-drink can in foil. ....

....You can make a metal cone with shiny cardboard or by wrapping plain cardboard in foil.

Lunar landscape

Lay down lots of foil candy wrappers to make a colorful lunar surface. Then build your own metal robots. Do they look like the ones on this page?

Metal washers ....

Pipe cleaners can be bent into all sorts of shapes. ....

Paper clips ....

KNOW YOUR STUFF
Recycling one aluminum can saves enough energy to run a TV for 3 hours.

Aha! Foiled again.

49

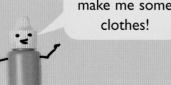
Somebody make me some clothes!

Fabric—it's in the clothes we wear!

It can be soft, furry, scratchy, strong, or stretchy. Yarns can be woven or knitted to make all kinds of garments.

Fabric

Imagine our world without fabric—we would probably catch a cold, since our clothes are made from it. Furniture is covered in fabric so it's soft and comfortable to sit on.

What is fabric made from?

WOOL comes from sheep, SILK from silk worms, COTTON from cotton plants, LINEN from flax plants. These are all natural products.

When was fabric invented?

The Egyptians first wove cotton into cloth about 14,000 years ago. The Romans built the first wool factory 1,500 years ago.

How is fabric made?

Fabric is usually woven from yarns like wool and cotton. Wool is sheared off the sheep (like a haircut), then spun into woolen yarn. Yarn can be woven into fabric—see page 56 to try weaving for yourself.

Lycra, nylon, and polyester

Fabrics like these are called synthetic because they are man-made. They are made in laboratories and are more like plastics than fabric.

How your fabric can help others

Take the clothes you've grown out of to thrift shops. They will not only be used by someone else, but they will also make money for charity, too.

Look for labels

Many clothes and other fabrics can be reused or recycled. Look at the labels—this one tells you the fabric is wool.

Recycling fabric

Remake clothes and fabric into something else. See the projects in this fabric section for some good ideas. If the fabric is falling apart, it can be made into filling for mattresses and insulation. So recycle your old towels, bed sheets, tablecloths, and curtains.

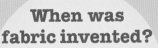

Making friends

They're woolly, they're soft, they're your fuzzy hat and glove friends! Have you grown out of your winter warmers? Then transform them into cuddly creatures.

KNOW YOUR STUFF
Sweaters and other items made of wool can be respun—the fibers are used again to make new clothes.

How to make woolly friends

Take a glove and decide what shape you want it to be. Turn to page 54 to find out how to do a back stitch, which will help you when you sew up the fingers.

1.

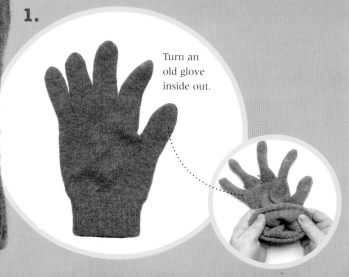

Turn an old glove inside out.

Make new friends from old

All kinds of gloves can be used—from baby mittens to Dad's big gloves. Experiment with how many fingers to use.

Try stuffing your old hats to make us!

I'm a glove with short fingers.

I've got a thumb nose.

.....Use all the fingers to make my hair.

2.

Sew up the middle two fingers and the thumb...

Turn the glove right side out again.

Push out the fingers that haven't been sewn up.

Cotton balls and old tights are great for stuffing gloves....

3.

Now make a face using stitches, fabric scraps, or buttons.

Stuff the glove.

Sew up the bottom.

Hold onto your hats!

Don't chuck them, recycle them.

Ask your family to give you their old hats. The more you have the more fuzzy folks you can make.

This bow came from a hat............

> Put a bow on your hat and make me— Betty Bow

What to use for stuffing

You can use almost any soft fabric for stuffing. Old socks and Mom's old tights and hose are probably the pieces of clothing people throw away most often, so gather them up before they go!

A quick sewing lesson

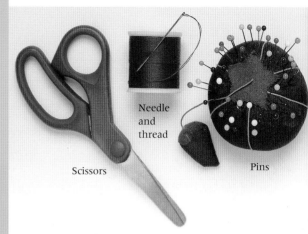

Scissors

Needle and thread

Pins

Back stitch

The back stitch is a good stitch to use because it keeps the stuffing in place. Practice on a piece of material before you sew the hats.

Knot the end of the thread and push the needle down and up through the fabric.

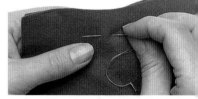

Pull the needle all the way through to the knot.

Now push the needle half way between the knot and the dangling thread.

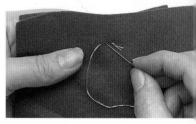

Bring the needle up in front of the dangling thread.

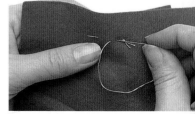

Repeat these steps and sew over the last stitch to finish off.

How to make Beanie Bob

Try to find two hats that are about the same size. Ideally, Bob should have one hat without a beanie, and one hat with a beanie. But you can always make your own pom-pom to go on top.

Find two hats, about the same size.

Old buttons

Sew on buttons or fabric scraps to make Bob's face.

6. Now make the face

1. Pin the hats together

Turn the top hat upside down.

Turn the bottom hat inside out.

Place the top hat into the bottom hat.

Pin the edges together.

Neatly sew up the opening.

5. Sew up the gap

2. Sew the hats together

Sew along the pins but leave a 5 in (12 cm) opening at the end.

Turn the hats right side out through the opening.

3. Turn right side out

Keep stuffing until Bob feels really full.

4. Stuff

Push your stuffing through the opening.

55

Rag mats

Revive old rags

Collect up material and old clothes, cut them into strips, and weave them into pretty mats.

Cut long strips of cloth 1 in (2 cm) wide.

To make strips longer, knot them together.

Cutting the strips

Cut the material into long strips. Use one color for the main weave that goes up and down, called the "warp," and lots of colors and fabrics for the "weft"—the material the goes across.

Use any old fabric.

How to start

Use a cardboard sheet for your weaving frame. Cut an even number of slits at the top and bottom. Knot together lots of the same color strips to make one very long strip.

12 slits

Cut the slits ½ in (1 cm) apart.

Cardboard sheet: 8 x 12 in (20 cm x 30 cm)

12 slits

Slip the fabric into the first slit.

Thread the fabric through each slit in turn, around and around from front to back.

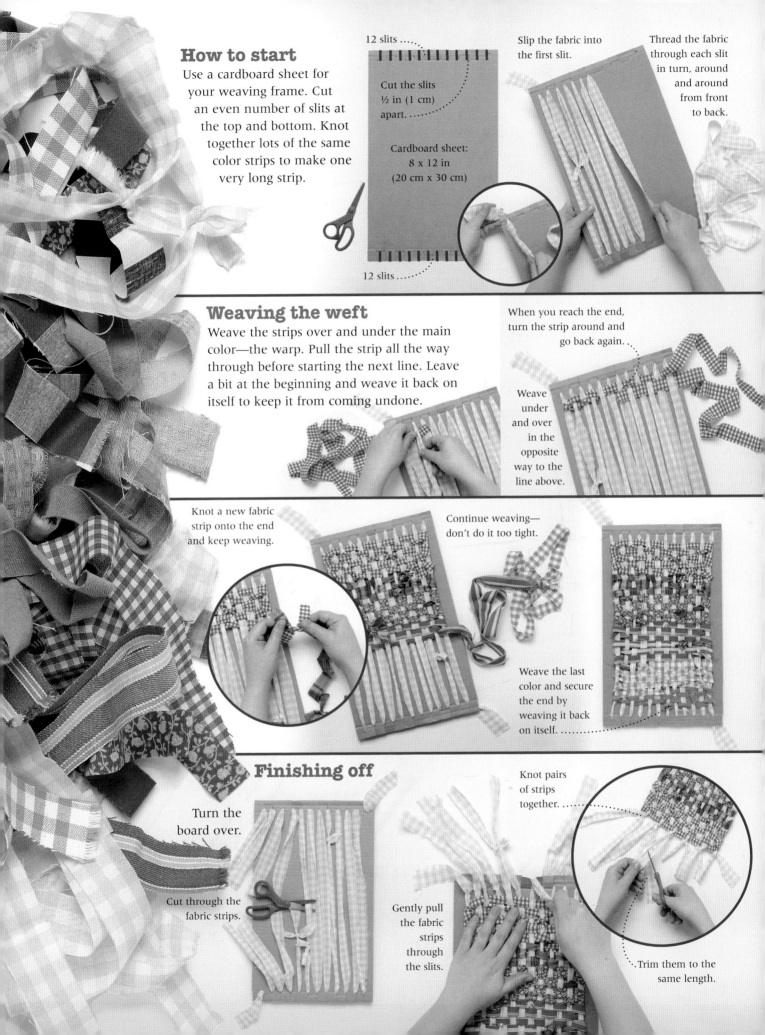

Weaving the weft

Weave the strips over and under the main color—the warp. Pull the strip all the way through before starting the next line. Leave a bit at the beginning and weave it back on itself to keep it from coming undone.

When you reach the end, turn the strip around and go back again.

Weave under and over in the opposite way to the line above.

Knot a new fabric strip onto the end and keep weaving.

Continue weaving— don't do it too tight.

Weave the last color and secure the end by weaving it back on itself.

Finishing off

Turn the board over.

Cut through the fabric strips.

Gently pull the fabric strips through the slits.

Knot pairs of strips together.

Trim them to the same length.

Pocket purses

Don't toss your old clothes, they might make perfect pocket purses!

I'm just right for a change purse!

Make a change purse

Look for an old piece of clothing with a pocket on the outside—one with a zipper or button is ideal. Cut around the pocket with pinking shears (scissors with zigzag edges) and you have your change purse—it's as easy as that!

Using pinking shears means that the edges won't fray.

Pinking shears

Pants purse
Rescue your favorite old jeans and turn them into these hip bags.

KNOW YOUR STUFF
Even when fabric is so worn out that it's falling to pieces, it's still worth recycling. It can be used for insulation and filling for mattresses.

Recycle your pants and skirts,

make glam bags for school...

...and change purses for pockets

Fabric

How to make a glam bag

Recycle old pants

to make these glamorous bags. Simply cut off the legs, sew up the opening, and attach a handle.

Needle, thread, and pins

1.

Cut off the pant tops just above the legs.....

2.

Turn inside out

Turn the top inside out and pin the two bottom edges together.

Sew the edges together.

3. Turn right way out

Pin the strap in place.....

Sew it tightly.

Use pinking shears with zigzag edges so the material won't fray.

Add a strap

Use the material from the leg to make your strap. Cut a length about 1 in (3 cm) wide and sew it in place.

Glam it up

When you have finished your bag, you can decorate it with beads, baubles, and bows. Then there are all those handy pockets to fill!

Make a matching change purse.....

Fancy strap

You could use a ribbon for the strap, like this pink velvet one.

Comfy cushions

Snuggle up to your favorite T-shirt or jeans after you have grown out of them. Brighten up your bedroom with these quirky cushions.

Clothing cushions

As well as reusing your T-shirts, try making glam bags (page 60-61) into cushions, too.

The pockets are still handy.

These look cozy—now you can enjoy your favorite clothes for longer!

KNOW YOUR STUFF

Most clothes that are thrown away are still good to wear. DON'T BURY THEM IN A LANDFILL. Give them to a charity.